Been to
BRAZIL

Annabel Savery

Facts about Brazil

Population: 184 million

Capital city: Brasília

Currency: Real (R$)

Main language: Portuguese

Rivers: Amazon, São Francisco, Paraná, Tocantins

Area: 8,511,965 square kilometres (3,286, 488 square miles)

 An Appleseed Editions book

Paperback edition 2014

First published in 2011 by Franklin Watts
338 Euston Road, London NW1 3BH

Franklin Watts Australia
Level 17/207 Kent St, Sydney, NSW 2000

© 2011 Appleseed Editions

Created by Appleseed Editions Ltd,
Well House, Friars Hill, Guestling, East Sussex TN35 4ET

Planning and production by Discovery Books Limited
www.discoverybooks.net
Designed by Ian Winton
Edited by Annabel Savery
Map artwork by Stefan Chabluk
Picture research by Tom Humphrey

ISBN 978 1 4451 3286 0

Dewey Classification: 981'.065

A CIP catalogue for this book is available from the British Library.

Picture Credits: Alamy Images: p11 (Holger Mette), p17 (imagebroker); Arthur Mota: p16; Corbis: p8 (Antonio Lacerda/EFE), p9 (Mike Theiss/National Geographic), p14 (Atlantide Phototravel), p15 (Jeremy Horner), p25 bottom (Wolfgang Kaehler), p26 (Sergio Moraes/ Reuters); Discovery Picture Library: p18 (Ed Parker); Getty Images: pp6-7 (Steve Allen), p13 bottom (SambaPhoto/Cassio Vasconcellos), p19 (Luis Veiga), p20 (Rolf Richardson), p24 (AFP), p29 (Nico Tondini); Istockphoto: p12 & p31 (Agenturfotograf), p21 top (luoman), p22 bottom (thejack); Nature Picture Library: p21 bottom (Mark Carwardine); Shutterstock: p2 (tristian quesnelle), p5 top (Dr Morley Read), p5 middle (gary yim), p10 (jbor), p13 top (Peter Leahy), p22 top (guentermanaus), p23 (guentermanaus), p25 top (ecoventurestravel), p27 (guentermanaus), p28 top (ostill); Wikimedia: p28 bottom (Cayambe).

Cover photos: Shutterstock: main (Elder Vieira Salles), left (ostill), right (Vinicius Tupinamba).

Printed in Singapore.

Franklin Watts is a division of Hachette Children's Books, an Hachette UK company.
www.hachette.co.uk

Contents

Off to Brazil!

We are going on holiday to Brazil.

Brazil is an enormous country in the continent of South America. There are high mountains and flat areas called plains.

There are also huge rainforests. We are going to many different places so there will be lots of travelling. I can't wait to go there!

Here are some things I know about Brazil...

• Brazil is the largest country in South America and the fifth largest in the world.

• The River Amazon is in Brazil. It is 6,480 kilometres (4,026 miles) long. It is one of the longest rivers in the world.

• There are lots of festivals in Brazil. These are big celebrations with music and dancing.

On our trip I'm going to find out lots more!

Arriving in Rio de Janeiro

From home we fly to Rio de Janeiro. This is a city on the eastern coast of Brazil. When we arrive, it is hot and sticky. We take a bus from the airport to the city centre.

We leave our luggage at the hotel and set out to explore. First we take the **cog railway** to the **summit** of a peak called Corcovado.

On the summit of Corcovado is a huge statue of Christ the Redeemer. At 38 metres (124 feet) high it towers above us.

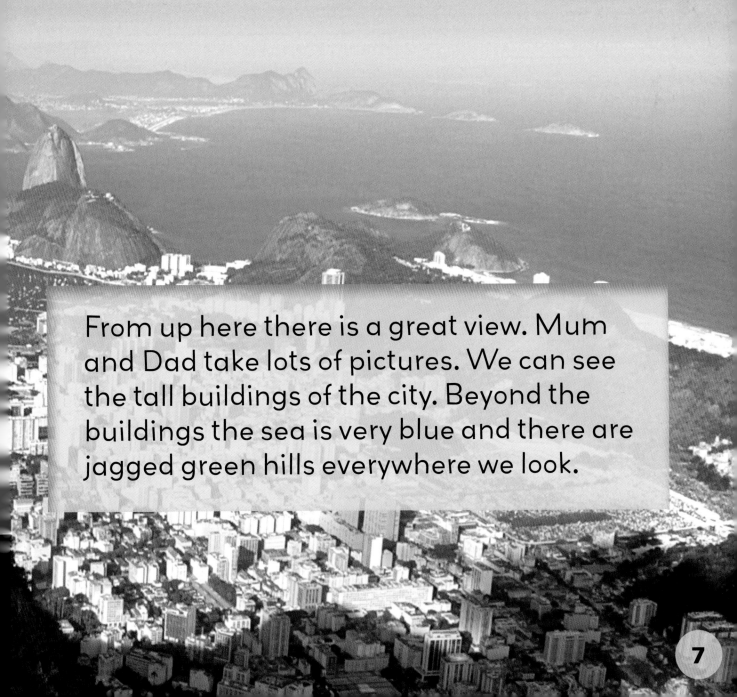

From up here there is a great view. Mum and Dad take lots of pictures. We can see the tall buildings of the city. Beyond the buildings the sea is very blue and there are jagged green hills everywhere we look.

Carnival time!

Wherever we go in Rio, people tell us about Carnival.

Carnival is a big celebration that is held every year. It lasts for four days and three nights. There are parades, shows, music and dancing. Carnival celebrates the time before **Lent** begins.

There are other festivals in Brazil too. Some are religious celebrations, others mark important days in the country's history, such as Independence Day.

Lots of people in Brazil are Roman Catholics. This religion was brought to Brazil by Portuguese explorers.

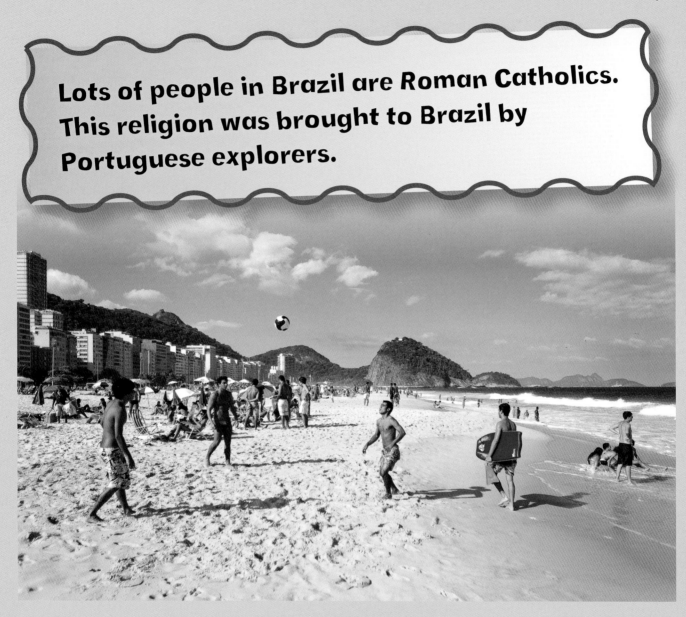

Before we leave we go to the beautiful Copacabana beach. There are lots of people here. Some are tourists on holiday, like us. Others are people who live in Rio and like to come here at the weekend. They are playing football and beach volleyball.

The next place we are going to visit is São Paulo city. It is the biggest city in Brazil. As we arrive, we can see tall skyscrapers.

There are lots of offices, and Dad explains that many businesses are based here.

The city is crowded. People from all over the world live in São Paulo. Many Europeans and Japanese people have come to live in the city.

The streets are busy. Some people are dressed for work; others are shopping.

People are selling food from stalls; some of them are children.

Children have to go to school from the age of seven to 14. However, some families are poor and their children miss school to work and to help earn money.

The Iguaçu falls

From São Paulo we fly to the town of Foz de Iguaçu. The Iguaçu Falls are nearby. They are on the border between Argentina and Brazil.

The Iguaçu Falls are amazing. The noise of rushing water is very loud.

The falls are made when the River Iguaçu falls over a sheer drop. At the top of the falls the river is four kilometres (2.5 miles) wide. When it falls it splits into 275 waterfalls!

The falls are in a national park.
Many types of wildlife live here.
Butterflies flutter about.
Toucans, monkeys, lizards
and deer live here too.

Further north from the falls on the River Paraná is the 8-km (5-mile) wide Itaipu dam. The dam creates hydroelectric power. It provides electricity for Brazil and Paraguay.

From the Iguaçu Falls we fly to Salvador. It is a busy, bustling city.

Salvador is on the coast and is an important port. Brazil **exports** many products from here, such as tropical fruit, cocoa and soya beans.

Women called *Bahianas* are selling food from big trays. They are dressed in traditional clothes.

We try *acarajé*. It is made from black-eyed peas that are rolled into a ball and deep-fried. Then this is split open and stuffed with spicy shrimp paste. Yum!

Lots of the food in Salvador has African origins. When the Portuguese first came to settle in Brazil they brought over African slaves to work on sugar plantations. African culture and traditions have been passed down to people who live in Brazil today.

Exploring Recife

Our next stop is the city of Recife. I like exploring Recife, but it is easy to get lost. The streets are narrow and winding. There are high, modern buildings, old-looking churches, and busy markets.

One of the markets is called the *Mercado São José*. Inside the stalls sell fish, meat and vegetables. Others sell handicrafts. Mum buys me a necklace made from seeds.

On the outskirts of the city the buildings are different. They are not tall and smart like in the city centre. Most are simple and small. These areas are called *favelas* or shanty-towns. People with little money live here. There are *favelas* in most Brazilian cities.

On the bus

Next we are going to travel to Belem. This is a city at the mouth of the River Amazon. It is going to be a long journey.

From Recife we have to catch two buses to get to Belem. The whole journey will take 36 hours!

On the way we travel through sugar plantations. Farming is important in Brazil. Mum says many crops are grown to feed the country's people and also to export.

Sugar cane

One fifth of Brazil's population work in agriculture. Most live in small villages in **rural** areas. They grow crops and raise livestock.

Coffee beans

One of the main crops is coffee. Brazil produces about a quarter of the world's coffee. It is grown in southern areas near São Paulo.

It is very hot and **humid** when we get to Belem. We are now very near the **equator**.

Belem is the port city of the Amazon. Boats come and go from here taking people and **merchandise** up-river. We are going to take a boat from here up the river to the city of Manaus.

We have a cabin on the boat. The journey is going to take five days. Mum has filled a basket with food for the trip, but there are meals served on board too.

The River Amazon is enormous. The area surrounding it is called Amazonia. This is made up of dense tropical rainforest and covers more than half of Brazil.

On the boat I look out for an Amazon River dolphin. In Brazil they are called *boutu vermelho*, which means 'red dolphin'.

The city of M--n--us

I feel a bit wobbly when we get off the boat in Manaus. Mum says it's because we've been moving for a long time.

Manaus is the capital of the state of Amazonas. There are high, modern buildings and traditional wooden houses. I am surprised to see such a big city in the rainforest.

At lunchtime we go to a restaurant. Fish is a popular food here and we all choose fish dishes. I have *caldeirada*. This is a fish and vegetable soup that originally came from Portugal.

In the evening we go to the *Teatro Amazonas*. It is a huge building with a coloured dome on the top and archways at the entrance. Inside it is decorated with patterns in bright colours.

In the rainforest

For a few days we are going to explore the rainforest around Manaus. Our guide is called Elso.

River Negro   **River Solimões**

First, Elso takes us to the place where two rivers meet, the Solimões and the Negro. The two rivers are different colours. The Solimões is yellow-brown and the River Negro is blue-black. Where they meet the two colours mix together.

Elso explains about the animals that live in the rainforest. They all sound strange to me. Fish called piranhas live in the river, as well as dolphins, alligators and **caimans.**

Caiman

Elso tells us about *caboclos* or 'the people of the forest'. They live in settlements near the river and have little contact with people who live in the cities. The *caboclos* know the forest very well and live on what they can find there.

As we leave we fly over more of the rainforest. It is a huge area. Dad says that there are some parts that have only been seen by people who live in the forest. They are no maps of these areas.

People explore the rainforest for different reasons. Some go to find out about plants. Others go to find out about people who live in the rainforest. Some scientists are even looking for new medicines in the rainforest.

There are **indigenous** Indian tribes who live deep in the rainforest. Some have no contact with the outside world.

There are areas where the trees have been cut down. Wood from the trees in the rainforest can be very valuable. People also clear land for buildings and growing crops. This harms the forest and the animals and people that live there.

The capital city

Our flight lands in Brasília, the capital city of Brazil. The government is based here. This is our last stop in Brazil.

In the afternoon we go to see the cathedral. It is made of lots of spikes in a circle. Inside, the beautiful roof is made of coloured glass.

A new city

Rio de Janeiro used to be the capital of Brazil. The government built the city of Brasília to encourage people to move inland. On 1 April 1960 the new city was opened and people moved in.

In the evening we go to a restaurant for our last meal before we fly home. I have *feijoada*. This is the national dish. It is made from black beans, pork, potatoes and herbs and spices. Feijoada is served with slices of orange. It is very tasty.

My first words in Portuguese

Many languages are spoken in Brazil. The most common and official language is Portuguese. There are words from other languages mixed in too.

Bom dia (say **Boom dee ah)**	Hello
Até logo (say **At-ay la-goh)**	Goodbye
Como vai? (say **Como vaai)**	How are you?
Como é seu nome? (say **Como ehy seo nameh)**	What is your name?
Meu nome é Antony. (say **Meo namay ehy Anthony)**	My name is Anthony.

Counting 1-10

1 **um/uma**   2 **dois/duas**   3 **três**

4 **quatro**   5 **cinco**   6 **seis**   7 **sete**

8 **oito**   9 **nove**   10 **dez**

caiman a reptile in the crocodile family

cog railway a type of railway that can travel up steep hills and slopes

equator an imaginary great circle around the Earth's surface. It is equal in distance from the north and south poles.

export to sell goods to another country

humid damp, moist air

hydroelectric able to produce electricity using moving water

indigenous people who originally come from a place

Lent the 40 days before Easter

merchandise products that are bought and sold in businesses

plantation an area where large amounts of a crop are grown in huge fields

rural in or near the countryside

summit the top of a hill or mountain

Index

Learning more about Brazil

Books

Brazil (Countries of the World) Brian Dicks, Evans Brothers Ltd, 2005.
Brazil (Discover Countries) Ed Parker, Wayland, 2009.
Brazil (World in Focus) Simon Scoones, Wayland, 2008.
Rainforest (Eye Wonder) Dorling Kindersley, 2004.

Websites

National Geographic Kids, People and places
   http://kids.nationalgeographic.com/places/find/brazil
Geography for kids, Geography online and Geography games
   http://www.kidsgeo.com/index.php
SuperKids Geography directory, lots of sites to help with geography learning.
   http://www.super-kids.com/geography.html